Also by Denise Loy Buchanan Ph.D.c.

Pamela the Palm Tree: Finding Strength in the Storms of Life
December 19, 2015; Live the Love Publishing
ISBN-13:978-0692596029; ISBN-10:069259602X
Children-Spirituality-Spiritual   Life-Metaphysics-Psychology-Philosophy-
Humanities-Educational
New Way Solutions (Illustrator)
Available on Amazon.com

Summary
Denise Buchanan grew up on the island of Jamaica where palm trees were prevalent
and so too were hurricanes. Denise has always been fascinated by nature and its
rich guiding principles which interweave with our life's journey and she unravels
in poetic verse, the story of Pamela the Palm Tree, who confronts a storm and what
it takes for her to emerge stronger in the end.

Wild
WISDOM

101 Inspirational Seed Thoughts
To Cultivate The Life You Love

Denise L. Buchanan, Ph.D.c

BALBOA
PRESS

A DIVISION OF HAY HOUSE

Balboa Press books may be ordered through booksellers or by contacting:

Balboa Press
A Division of Hay House
1663 Liberty Drive
Bloomington, IN 47403
www.balboapress.com
1 (877) 407-4847

Print information available on the last page.

ISBN: 978-1-5043-9567-0 (sc)
ISBN: 978-1-5043-9605-9 (e)

Balboa Press rev. date: 05/14/2018

Contents

Dedication

To the many teachers, guides, friends, clients, angels and seeming strangers whose Spirit danced and continues to dance with mine. These reflections are dedicated to you.

"If you truly love Nature, you will find beauty everywhere"
~Vincent Van Gogh

"If you wish to know the divine,
feel the wind on your face and the warm sun on your hand"
~Buddha

"Those who dwell among the beauties
and mysteries of the earth
are never alone or weary of life"
~Rachel Carson

Preface

"There is something of the marvelous in all things of nature"

- Aristotle

The spirit of peace, love, compassion, service, freedom and joy that yearns to seek expression in every human being is without a shadow of doubt my greatest muse. It is my passion to empower every individual to access their inner knowing which unleashes unlimited freedom, courage, peace and surprising treasures. I am committed that each person is fully engaged in the creation of an enlivened and amazing experience of life.

I have spent most of my life designing and creating Sacred Garden spaces in North America and the Caribbean. While it has brought me a tremendous amount of satisfaction to know I have created thousands of gardens, what I marvel at is the transformation of my sense of self as I worked on creating these garden spaces. What I found was the more time I spent in nature, the more I felt the hurts and disappointments I had carried through life melt away. I began to experience a deep peace and the feeling of being at home with myself which provided a key ingredient to connecting with others around me and with the vibrations of the earth. The inner expansiveness I encountered from listening to where a boulder wanted to be placed, or the urging from plants conspiring to be together or the observations of the unique venations on a leaf, these all led me to a place of deep gratitude for this gift of life and the communion with the divine grace in and through all things. The effortlessness, whimsical and sometimes dramatic occurrences which nature brings, continues to be thought provoking and highly instructive.

What is being activated when I experience these qualities in nature?

What is this connectivity I feel with nature and with life itself?

The exploration of these questions led me on a journey to discover that which exceeded my wildest expectations.

Acknowledgement

I am inspired by the many courageous individuals across the globe who despite life's challenges, get up each day with a renewed vigor to create a better world. I am especially encouraged by the fearlessness of those survivors and human rights activists who formed ECA: Ending Clergy Abuse, who have undertaken a tremendous global task to protect children from clergy abuse, especially in the Catholic Church. To Marek Lisiński, who set up the Do Not Be Afraid Foundation, Fundacja Nie lękajcie się; the only organization in Poland which helps victims of pedophile priests, you have my love and respect. I am heartened by Malala Yousafzai who along with her father Ziauddin, created the Malala Fund, an organization in Pakistan dedicated to provide all girls with an education. For the ingenious volunteers at The Hunger Project, a global organization committed to the sustainable end of world hunger, I support your vision of a world where every woman, man and child leads a healthy, fulfilling life of self-reliance and dignity.

I am grateful for the support and love of my colleagues worldwide who speak up against abuse of any kind and who hold the vision of a world of peace, justice, kindness and joy. For those who dwell in the possibility of creating a world that works for everyone, I stand with you.

Introduction

"There is in all visible things an invisible fecundity, a dimmed light, a meek namelessness, a hidden wholeness. This mysterious unity and integrity is wisdom, the mother of us all, "natura naturans." There is in all things an inexhaustible sweetness and purity, a silence that is a fountain of action and joy. It rises up in wordless gentleness, and flows out to me from the unseen roots of all created being welcoming me tenderly, saluting me with indescribable humility"

- Thomas Merton

Throughout time, the beauty and wonder of nature has infused itself into sacred texts, inspired writings and the spoken word. Notable volumes can be reviewed on the celebration of the natural order of things and I could easily spend many lifetimes immersed in the depth and breadth of inquiry and awe that nature evokes. In **Wild Wisdom** I was captivated by 101 inspiring quotes which took me on a nurturing wild mystical adventure through the four astronomical seasons. These seasons became the symbolic mirror of my sojourn through the stages of a difficult life to the greatness that was seeking to emerge. It is intended that these quotes and their accompanying personal reflections, when planted in your consciousness season after season, will activate something within you to expand your awareness of what's possible, realign yourself with the true nature of your being, spur action to cultivate your inner spiritual garden and reap a harvest of delight. My deepest desire is that **Wild Wisdom** provides gems and insights that will encourage, heal, and inspire you to live a life you love.

Let's describe the astronomical seasons.

Equinox

There are two equinoxes every year when the Sun shines directly on the equator and the length of night and day are almost equal. One is in March (Spring or Vernal Equinox) and the other is in September (Autumnal or Fall Equinox). The March equinox has been historically celebrated as a time of hope, growth, rebirth and many cultures celebrate Spring festivals such as Easter and Passover. The Fall Equinox is widely celebrated as a time of harvest and thanksgiving.

Solstice

Solstice in a Latin term derived from the word 'solstitium' meaning 'sun-stopping' or 'sun-standing." Today it is used to describe the moment the sun reaches its northernmost point from the earth's equator and is visible in the sky for the longest period (around June 21, Summer Solstice) or when the sun is at its southernmost point from the earth's equator and is visible in the sky for the shortest period (around December 22, Winter Solstice). Each of these seasons carry their own symbolic meanings and opportunities which we shall explore.

In **Wild Wisdom** we begin our journey in the Winter Season, where seeds lay seemingly dormant in the earth, then activity is seen in the Spring Season when seeds sprout new shoots which make their way above ground. By the Summer Season we observe the maturing of the plants and then relish in an Autumn Season of magnificent harvest. Here we grow!

CHAPTER 1

Winter Solstice

"Of all the wonderful things in the wonderful universe of God, nothing seems to me more surprising than the planting of a seed in the blank earth and the result thereof"

- Celia Thaxter

In the warmer parts of the world, seeds of various kinds can be grown year round. In cold, snow laden northern regions of say Alberta, Canada, Winter is a time which signals dormancy and slow chemical activity within most plants. The northern winter season provides us with the symbolism where we will start our journey. It invites us to symbolically go within, quiet the mind, and relish in the inner stillness. It embraces the opportunity to lay to rest frenzied activity, old habits, negative attitudes and unflattering thoughts and encourages us to create a fertile environment of hope and new beginnings. It is in winter where we can carefully plant new seeds and allow the magic of nature to unfold.

Quote 1:1

"A rock pile ceases to be a rock pile the moment a single man contemplates it, bearing within him the image of a cathedral"

- Antoine de Saint-Exupery

The nature of a seed is that it contains within itself the DNA possessing all the fundamental and distinctive qualities which are needed for it to become what it is designed to become. An East Indian mango seed for example, holds all the genetic code needed for it to become a fully developed East Indian mango tree with its far reaching branches, long slender leaves and fleshy juicy fruit. So too each of us has a dormant seed of majesty within us that is waiting to be unleashed so that we can develop and blossom into the full expression of what we were created to be. I am here on planet earth at this time for a purpose which can only be fulfilled by me. So too you are magnificently and wonderfully created for such a time as this to be a part of the movement to create a world that works for everyone. Consider that perhaps you are the one made to solve world hunger, eliminate homelessness or be the vanguard of loving families. What seeds then would you need to plant in your mind to bring this about? What must be uncovered and chiseled out to have the life you desire?

Quote 1:2

"Whatever words we utter should be chosen with care for people will hear them and be influenced by them for good or ill"

- Buddha

Each word that I speak represents a seed that I am planting into my consciousness and those of others. The moment I speak a word, it carries with it an energy that can uplift or destroy its intended or unintended target. A word can create a victory or lose the war. A word can provoke violence or calm fears. What seed did I just plant? What word did I speak into existence? Did I plant a seed that brought forth a harvest of the finest fruit or the sourest grapes? I am constantly invited to pay attention to each word. Much like ink injected into an ocean, once a word is released, it cannot be recovered.

Quote 1:3

"In the beginning was the Word, and the Word was with God, and the Word was God"

- John1:1 NIV

In the beginning of everything that is, was a decree that unfolded. Something is created out of the utterance of a word. Although a word is not a tangible thing or generally regarded as a no-thing, it is power-filled. The energy integrated into the no-thingness of words can form into whatever is intended and will move whatever is in the way to be what it needs to be.

Quote 1:4

"What we think, we become"

- Buddha

Before each experience, there is a thought that preceded it. As I take a close look at my own thoughts, I am aware that each thought I have is a group of words or pictures expressing an idea, view, opinion or conclusion about something or someone. When I consider that the experience I have of my life is a direct reflection of what I am saying to myself, then if I am not satisfied with the circumstances or happenings in my life, I have the opportunity to observe what I am saying to myself and change my thoughts. New thoughts will bring forth new experiences of the present even if my circumstances remain the same. In the same light, new thoughts of the present can provide a realm of possibility that can trigger new direction for action from which I can then change my circumstances.

Quote 1:5

"What lies behind us and what lies before us are tiny matters compared to what lies within us"
- Henry Stanley Haskins

The distinctive attribute of a seed is its inherent capacity for growth. So too the seed thought of my perception of myself will determine my growth into a greater expression of myself or my diminishment into a cynical minimalistic existence. I don't see a seed questioning its purpose. It just grows.

Quote 1:6

"The thing to do, it seems to me, is to prepare yourself so you can be a rainbow in somebody else's cloud. Somebody who may not look like you. May not call God the same name you call God - if they call God at all. I may not dance your dances or speak your language. But be a blessing to somebody"

- Maya Angelou

The soil of my mind can be cultivated so that the seed thoughts I am planting encourage constructive words to bloom anytime, anywhere, regardless of the situation. When I observe negative thoughts, I have the opportunity to see them as just that, negative thoughts passing through. Not reality. No need to pour fuel or fertilizer on them by dwelling on them so they magnify and take root in my consciousness. It is within my power to create the proper conditions that will allow the possibilities of life to emerge and be the person whose thinking results in words of upliftment and encouragement.

Quote 1:7

"The word devil is very beautiful, if you read it backwards it becomes lived. That which is lived becomes divine and that which is not lived becomes the devil"

- Osho

Each seed was designed with a protective coating which it must shed in order to grow into a full mature plant. The stirring from within, allows each of us to shed our protective coating that keeps us separated from the new life which is trying to emerge. This armor we created around our heart served its purpose in the past to protect us from feelings which may have resulted in us experiencing hurt and rejection. However, this armor hinders us from growing. If we lived the rest of our life protected, caged, afraid, anxious and worried what other people would think of us, or say to us, or do, we would miss the unexplored adventures and wondrous undertakings which are available ahead of us.

Quote 1:8

"You don't have to live forever, you just have to live"

- Natalie Babbitt

We were designed to be courageous, daring, bold and adventurous. We were created to grow and love with our whole heart. I declare that it's time for each of us to show up and be seen for the glorious expression that we are. What if Usain Bolt, Mother Teresa, Gandhi or Martin Luther King Jr. were too afraid to show us what was possible in life? The world is not waiting for another Bolt, Mother Teresa, Gandhi or King, the world is waiting for me and the world is waiting for you to reveal the gifts we were born to share. We are the solution to someone's suffering.

Quote 1:9

"Smooth runs the water where the brook is deep"

- William Shakespeare

As I think beyond the present conditions in my life, in the stillness of prayer and meditation or the observation of a flower or sunset, I can break free from lack, limitation and the turmoil of life. If even just for a moment, I can allow myself to see beyond my circumstances and touch the seed vision planted in my soul which is seeking to emerge through me.

Quote 1:10

"Unless a grain of wheat falls into the earth and dies, it remains just a single grain; but if it dies it bears much fruit"

- John 12:24 NIV

To be willing to quit the small insignificant games that stop me; to die to my old ways of being that don't serve me; to liberate my mind from mental slavery, is what is required to have a life that is filled with abundant gifts of joy, health, beauty and love.

Quote 1:11

"We have been created for greater things, to love and be loved"

- Saint Mother Teresa

What if a seed of love could be seen as the life force stirring in our soul. What if each soul around the world could stir another and cause the triumph over lifetimes of misinformation and patterns that create suffering in the world. What if we claim the connectivity between each of us and live as if each person mattered. Perhaps then we could proclaim the greatest victory planet Earth has ever known: A world that works for all.

Quote 1:12

"To forget how to dig the earth and to tend the soil is to forget ourselves"

- Mahatma Gandhi

Tending the soil of our consciousness with meditation, spiritual work, contemplation of the mysteries and awesomeness of life, pushes the boundaries of learned mediocrity and prepares the right conditions for the seeds of truth to flourish.

Quote 1:13

"For each tree is known by its own fruit. Indeed, people do not gather figs from thorn bushes, or grapes from brambles"

- Luke 6:44 NIV

If we keep thinking negative thoughts, we will keep getting negative outcomes. The reverse is also true. We have a choice to produce a life harvest of goodness or chaos, regardless of what trauma occurred throughout our living. Our thinking about the events in our lives gives us a life of victory or a life as a victim. Our choice.

Quote 1:14

**"Strength does not come from physical capacity.
It comes from an indomitable will"**

- Mahatma Gandhi

A seed planted in soil, facing harsh or optimal conditions, doesn't ask the question, what do I do now? It just grows.

Quote 1:15

**"Drop the idea of becoming someone, because
you are already a masterpiece.
You cannot be improved. You have only to come
to it, to know it, to realize it"**

- Osho

Look in the mirror and recognize that you are a work of outstanding artistry; unique, gifted, skilled, valued, important to the planet. Dwelling on this truth empowers you to be pulled by a vision of purpose. If you choose to diminish yourself, we all miss out on the difference you are here to make in this world. People don't determine your destiny. You do.

Quote 1:16

"To me, every hour of the light and dark is a miracle"

- Walt Whitman

How I choose to see the world is up to me. Do I curse the darkness and praise the light, or do I rest in the knowing that like a seed planted in the darkness of the soil, there is something being activated, something is being generated, something is occurring that will bring forth a new direction, a new sprout of understanding, a way forward.

Quote 1:17

"Though we travel the world over to find the beautiful, we must carry it with us or we find it not"

- Ralph Waldo Emerson

Let us allow the seeds of miracles to take root, seeing the magnificence of life all around us and expecting dreams to come true.

Quote 1:18

"All seasons are beautiful for the person who carries happiness within"

- Horace Friess

Our actions follow our thoughts and at times our pursuits may be constrained by seeming limitations. However, if we plant seeds in our consciousness of the truth of who we are as whole, complete, without blemish, holy, purpose filled, extraordinary, unique and remarkable beings and if we choose to constantly dwell on the beauty and brilliance that is breathing through us, as us, then we can set a new standard for living with a mindset filled with possibility and joy.

Quote 1:19

"Death and life are in the power of the tongue"
- Proverbs 18:21 NIV

We could describe the tongue as a weapon of mass destruction. How we use our tongue can damage friendships, stomp out seeds of dreams and ruin reputations. The tongue can also offer peace, prosperity, joy and life. You choose.

Quote 1: 20

"Change your opinions, keep to your principles;
change your leaves, keep intact your roots"
                                            - Victor Hugo

Would we welcome moments of challenge and change if we knew they would leave us with lessons from which we would grow into greater expressions of ourselves? Use these moments to allow your roots of faith and of goodwill to develop deep and wide so you can have a strong foundation to weather any storms that come your way.

Quote 1:21

> **"Everything you see has its roots in the unseen world. The forms may change, yet the essence remains the same"**
>
> *- Rumi*

Whatever I am committed to, shows up in my actions. If I am not experiencing the results I desire, it is a great opportunity to reflect on my thoughts operating in the background. Do I feel undeserving, inadequate, unloved or worried? To act on my purpose and intentions requires providing thought vitamins that will grow roots of vigilance, courage, resilience and power which will strengthen me to produce the outcomes I desire. Positive nourishment for our physical body, mind and spirit cultivates the best outcomes for our lives.

Quote 1:22

"Out beyond ideas of wrong doing and right doing there is a field. I'll meet you there"

- Rumi

Reveling in the unexplainable purity of nature, the seeds of truth within us can take root and be expressed. We are urged then to frequently take time away from the frenzied activity of life and spend time in the contemplation of the beauty that is around us so we may cultivate a life that gives welcome to the truth and blesses the world.

Quote 1:23

"I can't change the direction of the wind, but I can adjust my sails to always reach my destination"

- Victor Hugo

Seeds planted upside down will correct themselves and grow right side up. Difficulty was not made to stop us, it just provides the opening for us to correct our course.

Quote 1:24

"The roots of all goodness lie in the soil of appreciation for goodness"

- Dalai Lama

We have control over which seeds we allow to take root in the soil of our mind. Each moment we have the opportunity to guard our consciousness and dwell on that which brings forth good.

Quote 1:25

"**Every man is a doorway through which the Infinite passes into the finite, through which God becomes man, through which the Universal becomes individual**"

- Emerson

Each seed has a unique blueprint, infused with the creative impulse to express its divine nature and grow. The gift of life is proof that each of us is here to make a difference. Shall we make the best use of our time here or squander this precious gift?

Quote 1:26

"You realize that all along there was something tremendous within you, and you did not know it"

- Paramahansa Yogananda

You were born great with nothing to prove. Each moment presents the possibility of rediscovering the beautiful being that you see looking back at you in the mirror and then allowing yourself to grow into the majesty of your divine birthright.

CHAPTER 2

Spring Equinox

"Cheerfulness is the atmosphere in which all things thrive"

- Johann Paul Richter

The Spring Equinox has been historically celebrated as a time of hope, renewal and growth. At this time of year the harmonizing balance of the earth and the warming sun stimulate enzymes and microbial activity in the soil. Seeds are activated to send down deep roots which anchor new emerging plants. As the roots create a firm foundation, new shoots are pushed up through the soil and new life is revealed. So too the seed of divine consciousness within us is always alive even if it may be clouded by veils of misunderstanding and limited beliefs. Spring can be symbolic of allowing new ways to take root in our being; starting new projects, sowing new seeds and developing new ideas to act on. Also during the Spring Equinox we can take this time for Spring cleaning; clearing out the weeds and clutter smothering our inner garden and making room for our unique expression to reveal itself.

Quote 2:1

> "We've got this gift of love, but love is like a
> precious plant. You can't just accept it and leave
> it in the cupboard or just think it's going to
> get on by itself. You've got to keep watering it.
> You've got to really look after it and nurture it"
>
> *- John Lennon*

Self-love is a key ingredient in creating a life that you love. How often do we keep on doing things for others to the point of exhaustion thinking that is what life demands of us. Becoming stressed out, tired and sick in the service of others is not what we are called to do. We too are important and are deserving of our care and love. Self-love is not selfish. It is required for us to take time for ourselves to be fully able to be present for others. Can we truly give if our cup is empty?

Quote 2:2

"You wander from room to room hunting for the diamond necklace that is already around your neck"

- Rumi

The power and magnificence of the divine presence dwells within and looks back at you in the mirror. When you are still, what you are seeking reveals itself. Will you see your unique creation and take the time to allow if to fully express through you?

Quote 2:3

"The kingdom of God is within you"
                                        - Luke 17:21 NIV

Consider the magnificence of our human body precisely directing billions of electrical impulses throughout the brain and masterfully circulating trillions of blood cells throughout our veins. The intricacies of the body systems and dynamic life force present in each and every being is mind boggling. Perhaps, looking outside ourselves for answers in not the solution. Perhaps, an inner glance will reveal an internal world, with its varied landscape of emotions, feelings, and sensations that will provide a lens to the understanding that you are the one you have been waiting for.

Quote 2:4

"At the still point, there the dance is"

- T. S. Eliot

Spiritual practice, meditation and prayer allow us to experience the divine gifts of joy and peace which are our inheritance. How magnificent to take the time to touch the dreams in our hearts which are ready to burst into delightful expression.

Quote 2:5

"The greatest glory in living lies not in never failing, but in rising every time we fall"
- Nelson Mandela

If you knew without a shadow of a doubt that you were here to light up the world, would you hesitate to shine?

Quote 2:6

"It's one of the greatest gifts you can give yourself, to forgive. Forgive everybody"
- Maya Angelou

Forgiveness is for our liberation. Not forgiving can be like allowing weeds of regret, disappointment and hurt feelings to smother us and stunt our growth. Weeding our garden, like forgiving, gets rid of the constraints to growth and provides the release from the entanglement of past negativity. It gives room for life to emerge and allows access to new possibilities for living.

Quote 2:7

"What you are looking for is what is looking"
- St. Francis of Assisi

You are more powerful than you know. Does a seed know its entire potential? Unless it is given a chance to grow, all its potential remains locked up.

Quote 2:8

"Laughter is the sun that drives winter from the human face"

- Victor Hugo

Be more interested in love, kindness and joy for all, than in hate and revenge. You can respect someone's choices but you don't have to be sucked into their way of being if it doesn't resonate with you. You have the power to create the space which allows for everyone's greatness to arise.

Quote 2:9

"Friends are the flowers in the garden of life, beginning with a seed of trust, nurtured with laughter and tears, growing into loyalty and love"

- Nishan Panwar

Nurture the companions that join with you on the journey. Celebrate those who grow with you and allow those who fall away to have the space they need for their journey.

Quote 2:10

"There are more things in Heaven and Earth, Horatio, than are dreamt of in your philosophy"
- William Shakespeare

The seed of divine consciousness within us is always alive, even if it is clouded by feelings of doubt, fear, greed or envy. We have the reflective conscious power to engage our mind to transcend our limited beliefs, think new thoughts and experience life anew. Sometimes we may feel we are not making any headway towards what we want in life. In these times it is necessary to get our unconscious mind, which powerfully influences our judgements, feelings or behavior, to support our hopes and dreams instead of sabotaging them. Our work in doing this is to take time to meditate and pray and ask any unconscious non-supportive processes to come to the foreground of our mind so that we can heal them for our greater good. At the same time it is important to feed our unconscious with expectations of love, health and peace, which will faithfully reproduce what we are habitually thinking.

Quote 2:11

"If you don't like something, change it. If you can't change it, change your attitude"
- Maya Angelou

If we knew that everything is connected by a divine tapestry and we cannot separate ourselves from it, wouldn't we be more tolerant of one another?

Quote 2:12

"Just as treasures are uncovered from the earth, so virtue appears from good deeds, and wisdom appears from a pure and peaceful mind. To walk safely through the maze of human life, one needs the light of wisdom and the guidance of virtue"

- Buddha

We are all born with a force of energy within us which increases or decreases in vibration depending on our actions and intentions. With positive conscious and deliberate thought bathed in an attitude of gratitude, we can allow this energy to be available and useful toward meeting our goals. Having confidence that there are inner workings of divine grace always working on your behalf, will allow anyone to rest secure. Why then not stay at peace? Worrying does not change the outcome, it only causes you distress while you wait for the result.

Quote 2:13

"The invariable mark of wisdom is to see the miraculous in the common"
- Ralph Waldo Emerson

Stop breathing for 10 minutes and we most likely won't recover to tell about it. The life giving force of breath is often taken for granted. We can't see it or touch it, yet it is so vital to our existence. Pausing to acknowledge the seemingly small ordinary everyday things opens us up to a whole new world of living in gratitude.

Quote 2:14

"Be as a bird perched on a frail branch that she feels bending beneath her, still she sings away all the same, knowing she has wings"

- Victor Hugo

It takes courage to live life. What if we deeply knew without a shadow of a doubt that we were cared for, supported, anchored and nourished as we grew into our full expression of ourselves? We would sing, wouldn't we, even if out of tune.

Quote 2:15

"The greatest glory in living lies not in never falling, but in rising every time we fall"
- Nelson Mandela

My prayer today is to let my soul rise up from the soil of contentment and mediocrity and soar to new heights of gratitude, love and peace. I give up the pity-party, I forgive myself for judging myself and I celebrate the beauty and joy which extends itself to me from each smile, flower and sweet fragrance encountered throughout my day.

Quote 2:16

"You'll never find a rainbow if you're looking down"

- Charlie Chaplin

Today is a new day. Storms that held you back yesterday will dry out. Dreams are still alive waiting to be watered and fed to thrive. There need be no more doubt or compromise because we can allow new beams of energy to feed our destiny. The fullness of what we planted will soon be harvested.

Quote 2:17

"The soothing tongue is a tree of life, but a perverse tongue crushes the spirit"

- Proverbs 15:4 NIV

I can be trapped by my words but if I give life by what I say, then to speak success, victory and promises of good into my life will bring just that. My life will grow in the direction of my words.

Quote 2:18

"A human being is a part of the whole called by us universe, a part limited in time and space. He experiences himself, his thoughts and feeling as something separated from the rest, a kind of optical delusion of his consciousness. This delusion is a kind of prison for us, restricting us to our personal desires and to affection for a few persons nearest to us. Our task must be to free ourselves from this prison by widening our circle of compassion to embrace all living creatures and the whole of nature in its beauty"

- Albert Einstein

The life force which created the rhythms and cycles of nature is also our deep spiritual essence. Just as an orange seed planted in fertile soil produces a magnificent harvest of fruit, so too, the seeds of goodness, kindness, grace and charity, sown into life, return a hundredfold to fill our hearts with peace and joy.

Quote 2:19

"It is better to live your own destiny imperfectly than to live an imitation of somebody else's life with perfection"

- The Bhagavad Gita

Dare to live life full out, regardless of who is watching or not watching, regardless of handicaps and mishaps, regardless of fear and dread. Just live.

Quote 2:20

"If you truly love nature, you will find beauty everywhere"

- Vincent Van Gogh

Rising above thoughts of race, color, creed and identity we can experience our shared humanity and see the difference that a loving heart can make.

Quote 2:21

"The more clearly we can focus our attention on the wonders and realities of the universe about us, the less taste we shall have for destruction"
- Rachel Carson

Each day I let my soul surrender to that which is seeking to be revealed through me. I forgive, give forth and give up any thoughts of lack or limitation or persons or things which I allowed to hold me back. I am ready to take on what I have been created to be and do. I release my gifts and talents now. I declare I am a beneficial presence on the planet.

Quote 2:22

"When I admire the wonders of a sunset or the beauty of the moon, my soul expands in the worship of the creator"

- Mahatma Gandhi

My experience of life is my choice. The more I experience beauty and joy and love around me, the more fertilizer is available to nourish the soil of my being so that I may experience even more fully the growth of the miracle of life that is me.

Quote 2:23

**"Who you are thunders over you all the while so
that I cannot hear what you say to the contrary"**
- Ralph Waldo Emerson

Am I allowing heaven on earth to express through me or am I
caught up in myopic tendencies? Who I am being in any moment
will always precede any words I speak. If who I truly am is one here
to express my infinite potential, to be used by the divine presence
to express the highest vibration of love, peace, connection and
grace that was present before the beginning of time, my daily
practice is to tune into that frequency and allow it to direct my
everyday life.

Quote 2:24

"Trees are Earth's endless effort to speak to the listening heaven"

- Rabindranath Tagore

When I see the robust branches of a majestic tree towering above my head, I am called to stand tall, expand into the natural spaciousness of life and share that peace and joy with my brothers and sisters.

Quote 2:25

"You must not lose faith in humanity. Humanity is an ocean; if a few drops of the ocean are dirty, the ocean does not become dirty"
- Mahatma Gandhi

The divine essence of life would not have put a dream in your heart without a way to bring it to pass. I have a responsibility to pursue my dreams and talents because the world is waiting for my unique gift. As I uncover what I am here to do, it is important to surround myself with people who are growing along with me. Just because a few people may have offended me, that is not a license to give up and hate people. As I vibrate with love and peace on my journey, those with likeminded goals will gravitate towards me. We will find each other.

CHAPTER 3

Summer Solstice

"The indescribable innocence of and beneficence of Nature,--of sun and wind and rain, of summer and winter,--such health, such cheer, they afford forever!"

- Henry David Thoreau

In the Summer Season we see the maturing of the plant and the full development of what we planted. Summer symbolizes for us, a time of no secrets. We will no longer hide our truth or bury our talents. We now have the freedom to shine and express wholeheartedly. Whatever we planted is revealed. Our vitality is unleashed. Adventures await. We are present and the possibilities for success are endless.

Quote 3:1

"Our lives become beautiful not because we are perfect.
Our lives become beautiful because we put our heart into what we are doing"

- Sadhguru

If we could see the miracles that are occurring beneath our skin we would be in awe of the magnificence that we are. The gift is to have the faith of knowing that miracles are happening even if we don't see it.

Quote 3:2

"Do ordinary things with extraordinary love"
- Saint Mother Teresa

How fortunate we are to be able to live a life that provides opportunities at every turn to show kindness, to give a helping hand or give compassion. We could choose to be about the business of loving every day without thought for what we could get in return.

Quote 3:3

"Grace is not that has to descend from somewhere, Grace is there but if your doors are closed it is of no use"

- Sadhguru

Our subconscious mind can be running unhelpful patterns causing self-sabotage and chaos in our lives. How can we identify these patterns if they are hidden from view? One way is to be willing to see what shows up in life as gifts of grace, acting as mirrors of our inner selves. These mirrors will reveal the unhealed parts of ourselves. Just ignoring or covering up the problems that are revealed will not make them go away, just like trimming the branches of a tree will not fix the tree if the roots are rotten. What is needed is an extraction of those thoughts rooted in our consciousness which produce negativity, turmoil and pain. When new thought plantings of joy, courage, vigor and upliftment, are allowed to take root, these will ignite new possibilities for our life to flourish.

Quote 3:4

"It does not matter if you are a rose or a lotus or a marigold. What matters is that you are flowering"

- Osho

Each of us has been given a unique unlimited light beaming with love and grace that is readily available to shine into the world so that people may see what's possible for their lives. This inner light is always shining. Uncover it, be willing to stand on it and in it, so it may show you the way. Drop any judgements, misgivings, irritations, guilt or shame, for these attitudes are weapons you use against yourself. Forgive all who hurt you and situations that did not work out. Forgiveness is the gift you give yourself which will wipe away distortions of truth and thoughts of separation. It will lift your mind into peace and reveal more of your inner light which you can give to the world.

Quote 3:5

"But look around at this world, how perfectly it's made. Flowers can't move, yet the insects come to them and spread their pollen. Trees can't move either, but birds and animals eat their fruit and carry their seeds far and wide"
- Nahoko Uehashi

Who we are being sends ripples through the Universe. If we are feeling tied to the world's definition of success then we may be stuck in a forever frenzy chasing dreams of more stuff which will consume us and leave us feeling empty. However, if we gather new perceptions of the world such as one which is supportive of our work or as one that is being healed, there arises a future very different from the past. We can choose to use the present to be free. If we are interested in being a part of the flow of life that welcomes peace and truth, we can focus on this light filling our being and the magnetic power of this vision will pull towards us more of that which we desire.

Quote 3:6

"Remember, in the vast infinity of life, all is perfect, whole, and complete...
and so are you"

- Louise L. Hay

As we grow, there is the freedom to live fully without the need or desire to be fearful of what might be or what might come about. It is not a license to be reckless but an inspired desire to fully express all that we were created to be.

Quote 3:7

"**Nobody else can destroy you except you; nobody else can save you except you. You are the Judas and you are the Jesus**"

- Osho

Dwell on the seed ideas that you desire to take root in your consciousness. Pluck out the weeds, which are the thoughts that do not support you, for they too produce seeds which if allowed to root, will crowd out your dreams.

Quote 3:8

**"Gratitude is not only the greatest of virtues,
but the parent of all the others"**

- Marcus Tullius Cicero

Whatever you feed grows. Feeding sad thoughts with more regret, guilt, blame or shame will only cause them to grow larger. Spending your energy dwelling on insecurities or doubts is watering that which you don't want in life. However, dwelling on thoughts that inspire: giving thanks each day for the air that we breathe or the blessings all around us, sets in motion an ancient spiritual law that the more you are grateful for, the more will be given to you.

Quote 3:9

"It is not in the stars to hold our destiny, but in ourselves"

- William Shakespeare

We are the ones to determine if we succeed or fail. We are the ones that choose to feed ourselves nourishing thoughts or junk food. It is time to starve the fears and quit reinforcing the insecurities and instead direct our energy into fortifying ourselves with confidence, strength and unlimited energy.

Quote 3:10

**"If we all did the things we are really capable
of doing, we would literally astound ourselves"**
- Thomas Edison

Unlimited potential lies dormant inside us. We have the incredible ability to retrain our mind to focus on that which will elevate our consciousness to bring us a life of our deepest desires. The other path is that we could allow the past hurts and regrets to take over, arrest our development and cause a lifetime of anguish of never having tried to go for our dreams. We have the power to choose onto which pathway we will take our life. Choose wisely.

Quote 3:11

"May your choices reflect your hopes, not your fears"

- Nelson Mandella

You may think you have a valid reason to feel resentful but directing your energy into this feeling tone will only bring more resentment. Where focus goes, energy flows to bring us more of what we focus on. Stop watering these weeds of resentment and refocus your energy towards what you want to grow more of in your life. Will you spend your life mourning the past, regretting what didn't work out; wishing things were different? You may mourn for a season, even though you know that you can't change the outcome, but then it is time to let go of what did not work out and move towards what you want in your life. A new season of joy and fulfilment in life awaits you with every new thought in that direction.

Quote 3:12

As my mind can conceive of more good, the barriers and blocks dissolve.
My life becomes full of little miracles popping up out of the blue"

- Louise L. Hay

Each day we have a chance to reset and redirect our energies to what's possible for our lives. Our dreams are alive, ready and waiting to be watered and fed in order to thrive.

Quote 3:13

"The happiness of your life depends on the quality of your thoughts"

- Marcus Antonius

You may believe that you are responsible for what you do, but not for what you think. The truth is that your behavior follows from the thoughts that you have allowed to root in your consciousness. You are responsible for these thought seeds because it is only at this level that you can exercise choice. What you choose to plant affects the quality of your life.

Quote 3:14

"The greatest mistake you can make in life is to be continually fearing you will make one"
- Elbert Hubbard

The past is behind us. We cannot grow into a new season of our lives if we are dwelling on and judging what's already done. Betrayals and difficulties happen. We cannot heal if we are constantly uncovering the scab and watering the weeds of our history. In our preoccupation with the past, we miss out on the new opportunities available to us. Yes, it is important that we learn the lessons from our previous missteps, but it is more important to move forward and plant new seeds in order to cultivate a rich new harvest. Past performance need not lead the way for future possibility. Each moment we can push the reset button and create fresh thoughts and new actions.

Quote 3:15

"Three things cannot be long hidden: the sun, the moon, and the truth"

- Buddha

The miracle of life is that it seeks to constantly express itself. Like a seed planted in the soil, even if we don't see it, it is there. Just as when the sun is concealed by the clouds or the moon is eclipsed, it is still there. The inner truth of who we are as divine beings having a human experience is still there even though we may busy ourselves with life's worry and doubt. If we want to reveal the truth, remove the clouds, stop doubting and worrying and be still. In the Zen tradition, the mind is described like a glass of cloudy water. If you want to clarify the water, stop shaking, stirring, and fussing.

Quote 3:16

> **"If you bring forth what is within you, what you bring forth will save you. If you do not bring forth what is within you, what you do not bring forth will destroy you"**
>
> *- Gospel of Thomas*

We were born whole and complete with everything we need within us to thrive. We all have something that must be brought into the world to fulfil our purpose; be it a dance, a social movement, a speech or something else uniquely ours. The greatest tragedy is that the world will be deprived of our contribution if we choose not to share what we have been given. If we choose to ignore and bury our gift, our aliveness diminishes and the energy it takes to quell our innate expression will seek ways to manifest usually in destructive ways to our mental and physical being. Similarly, with any hurt we have experienced, we need to get out of our own way and face what needs to be healed or else the hurt energy will find places to coagulate in our body and disrupt the natural functioning of the body temple. Illness and disease is largely unexpressed energy trying to get our attention so we may redirect our lives to a state of full expression, balance and harmony.

Quote 3:17

"There is one spectacle grander than the sea, that is the sky; there is one spectacle grander than the sky, that is the interior of the soul"
- Victor Hugo

Connecting with the vast interior spaciousness of our being provides the fuel for our aliveness. If we learn to navigate the world from the realm of our highest creation, the view of our circumstances will change. Our task is not to fight against our current situation because that only brings more of the same. Fighting war with war brings more war, not peace; fighting sickness without looking at the thoughts that brought on the sickness, only magnifies the sickness. Our work then is to cultivate the inner conditions we are seeking which will release us from the fight and dis-ease. It may seem strange that a shift in our perception will create this result but if we realize that our thoughts determine things, changing our thoughts will set in motion unseen processes that spur actions towards creating an outcome that matches our vision.

Quote 3:18

> "I believe we create our own lives. And we create it by our thinking, feeling patterns in our belief system. I think we're all born with this huge canvas in front of us and the paintbrushes and the paint, and we choose what to put on this canvas"
>
> *- Louise L. Hay*

How wonderful to know that in each and every moment I have the power to generate my own joy. Regardless of any dire circumstance I find myself in, regardless of my past disappointments, I can adjust my focus and see the beauty in the tall trees, breathe in the fragrance of nearby roses and celebrate good health. I can feel into the dreams I want for my life and take one step each day in the direction to their fulfilment. Once there is life, it is never too late to reset my inner compass and change my mind about what I think I deserve. I am the artist and I get to choose to begin newly to paint a beautiful life.

Quote 3:19

"Darkness cannot drive out darkness; only light can do that. Hate cannot drive out hate; only love can do that"

- Martin Luther King, Jr.

Human beings can engage in cruel, evil and hateful behavior. Hatred of the evildoer does not diminish hate, it increases it. By hating someone who is engaged in evil, you contribute to the evil and bring suffering on yourself. The presence of evil is simply the absence of light, for evil and light cannot coexist. The remedy for an absence of light is to introduce light. The more people that release themselves from hate, the less hate there will be on the planet. There is much in the world that we may consider to be evil: the abuse of children, the plunder of nations; we are called to do what we can to protect the children and give aid, but not from a place of hating those that do evil, because we then contribute to the perpetuation of the same. By acting out of compassion, the greater good can emerge, which fuels the light of change to shine on the situation. The more light we shine, the more darkness we can transform and the more good we can allow to grow on the planet.

Quote 3:20

"You must take personal responsibility. You cannot change the circumstances, the seasons, or the wind, but you can change yourself. That is something you have charge of"

- Jim Rohn

Summer reminds us of the vitality and youthfulness present in everyone's heart and soul no matter our chronological age. Regardless of the hurt, despair and fears we experienced, nothing is accomplished from blame and regret. There is no reward for holding anyone to ransom. We have the power to leave the past in the past and choose joy, choose to be happy, choose to take on life as a new adventure. Why not choose to experience love and beauty every day? That certainly will make us have a more satisfying encounter with life.

Quote 3:21

"Beauty is the only thing that time cannot harm. Philosophies fall away like sand, creeds follow one another, but what is beautiful is a joy for all seasons, a possession for all eternity"

- Oscar Wilde

Appreciating the beauty of nature provides access to the infinite nature of God. As I observe the elegance of a flower and keep my thoughts on the majesty of a tree, I partake in a profound testimony to the mysterious dynamic realms of creation and creativity within me.

Quote 3:22

"The need of expansion is as genuine an instinct in man as the need in a plant for the light, or the need in man himself for going upright. The love of liberty is simply the instinct in man for expansion"

- Matthew Arnold

As we grow we may need to release people in our lives who no longer support our growth and development. It is no accident that they walked with us, even for a season as we learned from each other. We appreciate them, bless them and love them from a distance. It is perfectly fine to be lonely for a season. Enjoy your own company. Take the time to strengthen your roots and expand the depths of your inner world so your vibration will attract into your life your next teachers and adventures in learning.

Quote 3:23

"So plant your own gardens and decorate your own soul, instead of waiting for someone to bring you flowers"

- Jorge Luis Borges

We have the opportunity each day to cultivate our own garden by enjoying our accomplishments, celebrating our victories and acknowledging our successes. As we honor ourselves, we plant healthy seeds which take root and prosper. Any limited beliefs in ourselves or our abilities are transcended; we use them as fertilizer to allow our lives to flourish.

Quote 3:24

"Ever since happiness heard your name it has been running through the streets trying to find you"

- Hafiz

The joy that comes from knowing that each of us is a unique creation, wonderfully made, whole and complete, loved, cherished and honored, brings a perpetual smile to my lips and an ecstatic dance to my soul. Knowing that angels hover all about each of us, comforting us, directing our every step, warms my heart. My mind is stamped newly with my indelible timeless value and as I know that to be true for me, I know that is true for you too and I trust in the all-encompassing power of good that dwells in our soul.

Quote 3:25

"The best remedy for those who are afraid, lonely or unhappy is to go outside, somewhere where they can be quiet, alone with the heavens, nature and God. Because only then does one feel that all is as it should be"

- Anne Frank

I look back at the times when I felt tormented, jealous and fearful and remember the emptiness I felt in my heart. I now know I was fooling myself with the lies about not being lovable, or good enough, or deserving of good things. I was imprisoning my wondrous spirit. In the garden, I felt that the birds sensed my sadness and conspired to sing a song just for me, I welcomed the breeze softly comforting my cheeks and the leaves of the trees applauding my very presence. In the garden I felt an indescribable presence which restored my heart. In the garden, I felt God.

CHAPTER 4

Autumn Equinox

**"I thank You God for ... this amazing day:
for the leaping greenly spirits of trees and a
blue true dream of sky;
and for everything which is natural which is
infinite which is yes"**

- e.e. cummings

The Autumn Season is a time of magnificent harvest. It is the season where we have the culmination of the seeds we planted and the revelations of the blessings and fruits of our labor. Autumn is also a time of renewal when leaves change color and fall from trees forming mulch which produces fertile soil into which seeds can take root. We can reflect on those things which we had to shed in order for us to have a life we desired. We celebrate our transitions and acknowledge our efforts that we fulfilled on and the provisions we have been afforded. What did we have to transform to make room for the newness that was calling us forth?

Also during the Autumnal Equinox we generally have night and day being the same length. This activity is symbolic of the concept of balancing the light and the dark aspects within ourselves. Life is a mixture of emotional experiences and as we move towards the light, we are called to respect the lessons provided by the dark times in our lives. Light and dark are two polarities of the same energy like day and night. One is not negative and one is not positive. They both contribute to the whole. The key in this season is finding balance or wholeness within your own world by tuning in to yourself and integrating your light and dark nature.

Quote 4:1

"The winds will blow their own freshness into you, and the storms their energy, while cares will drop off like autumn leaves"

- John Muir

Once we get out of our own way by letting go and giving up what no longer serves us, we can create a spaciousness within our being where we can now allow a download of creative energy to flow through us to fuel a more loving expression of ourselves.

Quote 4:2

"To love beauty is to see light"

- Victor Hugo

Observing nature shows us how to break free from our smallness and expand into the greatness that is our birthright. As we plant seeds of success, love and joy and nurture them, they take root in our consciousness. In order to flourish, we need to weed our garden of negative thinking and surround our mind with the fertilizer of truth that all things are working together for good. We can allow our vision of the soil of the world to take on a bright future as we see with new eyes the new plants emerging from the darkness and the beauty that is seeking to emerge.

Quote 4:3

"Blessed is the season which engages the whole world in a conspiracy of love"
- Hamilton Wright Mabie

The changing nature of life presents us with new mysteries every day. In this season, the unusual weather patterns and the spectacular foliage display personify these unknowns. If we accept that life is filled with adventures and unknowns, we will have more freedom and wonderment to develop the capacity to maneuver through life's ebbs and flows and live life to the fullest.

Quote 4:4

**"Every moment and every event of every man's
life on earth plants something in his soul"**
- Thomas Merton

During Autumn, especially in colder climates, animals prepare for Winter by storing food and readying themselves for hibernation. Farmers harvest their crops and retreat indoors. We tend to think of this time as a time of preparation for Thanksgiving holidays by cultivating a safe and comfortable home to reconnect with family and friends. It is also a time for us to reconnect with ourselves by consciously gathering and celebrating our blessings. The more gratitude we plant into our awareness, the more fertile the soil of our mind becomes to grow the seeds of our dreams.

Quote 4:5

"The life given us by nature is short, but the memory of a life well spent is eternal"

- Cicero

Autumn reminds us that our bodies, minds, and surroundings are always developing. Leaves function throughout the year to help plants produce food by converting the energy in sunlight into food the plants can utilize. These essential leaves now fall away in Autumn helping us to reflect on the impermanence of life, the remarkable nature of the present and the beauty of letting go.

Quote 4:6

"Change every quality in your heart to become a new quality full of light"
                                    - Sidi Muhammad al-Jamal

When we develop the habit of taking time to be silent and focus our awareness in our heart, there becomes a moment when there is no difference between our physical thoughts and our heartbeat. In that state we remember our divine nature and touch the unlimited potential that is our life.

Quote 4:7

"What we plant in the soil of contemplation, we shall reap in the harvest of action"

- Meister Eckhart

My thoughts can frighten me and in an instant I have the power to change them and exchange each fear thought for a happy thought that uplifts my spirits and brings me joy and love, regardless of the circumstances around me. I am the one that chooses what seed thoughts to plant in my consciousness. I am the one that cultivates the garden of my awareness, so it's best that I plant the seeds that I desire in order for me to have the intended outcome. Planting an orange tree seed expecting a harvest of mangoes is foolish.

Quote 4:8

> **"Everything has seasons, and we have to be able to recognize when something's time has passed and be able to move into the next season. Everything that is alive requires pruning as well, which is a great metaphor for endings"**
>
> *- Henry Cloud*

A garden constantly needs tending for it to grow at its best. Sometimes the action of cutting back dead braches and pruning back roses or grape vines seems drastic and we may wonder if we've gone too far. But oftentimes it is just this pruning that is required to get a more abundant crop of grapes or flowers in future seasons. Are there things in your life that you need to cut out or prune back in order for your life to work better? Perhaps you need to cut out certain unhealthy habits, walk away from toxic people or weed your mind of negative thoughts. What needs pruning or shaping in you?

Quote 4:9

> **"Nature's beautiful dancers — flowers, water, leaves dancing to the music of God's sweet breeze"**
>
> *- Terri Guillemets*

After all the work you put into your garden throughout the year, your garden should produce a bountiful crop, ready to be picked. Similarly, if focused and intentional; a good life plan will produce bountiful rewards: you'll be happy, healthy, enjoying your career, blessed with financial security, good relationships and awesome memories. You will rejoice in your blessings and honor the challenges. However, even if your harvest wasn't as bountiful as you would like it to have been and your life did not flourish as you planned, then regroup, redirect, reconnect and try again. All we are ever asked to do in life is keep believing in ourselves.

Quote 4:10

"Adopt the pace of nature: her secret is patience"
- Ralph Waldo Emerson

Patience is one of the greatest gifts we can give to another human being and to ourselves. By being patient with ourselves, we take the time to discover and appreciate our unique expression. By being patient with others, we allow them to just be themselves without us imposing our demands on them or stifling their creativity. As we freely allow people to be themselves, we provide space for them to grow and in so doing we grow ourselves.

Quote 4:11

> **"The true measure of a man is not how he behaves in moments of comfort and convenience but how he stands at times of controversy and challenges"**
>
> *- Martin Luther King Jr.*

It always amazes me to see a plant growing up through a crack in the concrete pavement. The urge to express life fully, despite obstacles is miraculous. Challenges provide the opportunity for us to grow into our most courageous, strong, confident and expansive selves. Difficulties give us the choice to allow them to make us stronger or we can allow them to beat the aliveness out of us. We may seek to take the safe known path in life without risks, but how does that teach us anything new about ourselves, how does that cause us to grow, how does that show us what we truly are made of? Stepping out in courage allows us to find the crack and grow through the concrete and trust in the directives of our heart's true nature.

Quote 4:12

"Nature does not hurry, yet everything is accomplished"

- Lao Tzu

With every season, there is change. This change in nature is consistent and effortless, yet sometimes fraught with storms and natural disasters like the journey of life itself. To get the full benefit provided through all seasons, nature teaches us to be mindful of what needs to be done and to be deliberate in doing it thoroughly and well until the task is accomplished. Then nature delights in pressing repeat.

Quote 4:13

"I love to think of nature as an unlimited broadcasting station, through which God speaks to us every hour, if we will only tune in"
- George Washington Carver

What we focus on is what we attract, so it is important for us to not focus on what is not working in our life. Yes, we can acknowledge what is happening when nature did not present us with a smooth road, but it serves no purpose to constantly lament on what's not working. If we choose to look, the ups and downs in life bring us lessons from which we can learn and grow. Our constant prayer should then be, God show me what this is for?

Quote 4:14

**"Take a walk outside - it will serve you far more
than pacing around in your mind"**
- Rasheed Ogunlaru

Quit minimizing your greatness. You were created with the genius stoke of love that permeates throughout nature. See the thousands of leaves on a tree and know that each one is uniquely different from the other. No two flower petals are exactly alike; no two rose bushes flower and grow in the same way. What good then does it make to complain of and negatively compare our tallness or shortness, our curviness or slimness, or the color of the skin of our body temple? Each of us is uniquely made, whole, complete, without blemish, gifted and designed to celebrate the masterful creation of life. The directive of life broadcasts to us: Just Be Great!

Quote 4:15

> **"The river is one of my favorite metaphors,
> the symbol of the great flow of Life Itself. The
> river begins at Source, and returns to Source,
> unerringly. This happens every single time,
> without exception. We are no different"**
>
> *- Henry David Thoreau*

Each day we can take a few moments to reap that inner harvest of peace and stillness which is the Source from which we came. The stream of consciousness available in those moments connects us to the truth of ourselves and the world of possibility is reflected back to us. Thoughts of separation vanish, seas of negativity evaporate and that which we seek emerges from within.

Quote 4:16

"You are as God created you. All else but this one thing is folly to believe.
In this one thought is everyone set free"
- A Course in Miracles

It is time to shed the insane notions that you are anything but magnificent. If you deny who you are as a divine being having a human experience, the pressures and constraints of this world will seem like a burden to endure alone and despair and hopelessness will creep into your consciousness. It is the season to look anew and see that you are a holy creation, free and powerful to create the life you desire. Your thoughts direct your harvest. By freeing yourself from your limited beliefs, you now have space to receive the fullness of life and in the same moment you then become available to be the catalyst to help someone else live a life they love.

Quote 4:17

> "There are mystical, unbreakable bonds between all members of the natural world including humans and animals. Whether or not we remember or acknowledge this relatedness, it still exists"

- Elizabeth Eiler

Any feelings of discouragement or defeat can be shed and used as compost from which we can fertilize the soil of our consciousness of possibility and connectivity. We can heal the separation in the world once we release our judgements and fears and take the time to see with new eyes the true nature of what this world is about. If we knew that our deep spiritual nature, our life force is in and through all living things and that we are divinely connected, would we be so quick to harm one another and destroy the planet?

Quote 4:18

> **"Love means to realize that we are one with life. Real love means to realize that we are one with the other person, one with nature, and one with the trees, the stones, the earth and the blue sky. It means to realize that all of life is God"**

- Swami Dhyan Giten

What if we deeply considered our inter-relatedness with other living forms on earth. Would we not then cultivate a reverence for the life of all creatures and our dependence on one another and be mindful of our place in nature–not as rulers over it, but as participants in it?

Quote 4:19

"Keep close to Nature's heart... and break clear away, once in awhile, and climb a mountain or spend a week in the woods. Wash your spirit clean"

- John Muir

There is something magical about walking in a forest or a park with large trees. Here I find all my anxieties melt away as if they are being absorbed by nature. As I breathe in the fresh air and listen to the leaves of the trees rustling overhead, I am reminded to stay in the moment and receive the gifts that are offered there. I know that whatever season of life I am in, or you are in; whatever challenge I am facing or you are facing, one thing is certain, change is inevitable. Our role is to assimilate and transform through the seasons, leave behind what no longer works and be available for what wants to be expressed through each of us.

Quote 4:20

"One touch of nature makes the whole world kin"
- William Shakespeare

What's the forecast for your life? Doom and gloom, clouds and rain, or sunshine and warm breeze? You choose which broadcast comes to life.

Quote 4:21

"I believe in God, only I spell it Nature"
                                    - Frank Lloyd Wright

The experience of the celestial breathing of nature and the yawning of the unfurling rose whisper of the marvelous miraculous mysteries in the quest to discover God. To this I listen, and not to the naysayers who prefer to squeeze out any seeds of possibility from my being.

Quote 4:22

"The day of the sun is like the day of a king. It is a promenade in the morning, a sitting on the throne at noon, a pageant in the evening"
- Wallace Stevens

Each season has its challenges and difficulties, growing pains and lessons. Fall brings to our consciousness the changing nature of everything and challenges us to be present and acknowledge each and every moment because the things and people we love will not be around forever.

Quote 4:23

"The sun, with all those planets revolving around it and dependent on it, can still ripen a bunch of grapes as if it had nothing else in the universe to do"

- Galileo Galilei

As we learn and evolve through the seasons of life, the attention to the miraculous inner functioning of even the smallest creature and process of nature attests to the highest precision of a divine hand at work in every moment. For this I am grateful.

Quote 4:24

"**The purpose of life is undoubtedly to know oneself. We cannot do it unless we learn to identify ourselves with all that lives. The sum-total of that life is God**"

- Mahatma Gandhi

Feelings are the means through which we connect with another and through which we can discern the parts of ourselves that the soul seeks to heal. Through our feelings we can experience the action of the soul manifesting in physical matter. It is important not to judge events or our circumstances, even if they seem difficult. We do not know the greater divine plan that is at work; we do not know what is being healed or the energetic balance that is emerging. We must allow ourselves to feel the compassion that arises from these circumstances and direct our energy towards cultivating thoughts and actions that will transform circumstances and create balance and reverence for life, rather than more violence and ill-will. If we immerse ourselves in compassion, we will feel the interdependence of all living beings, connected and vital in bringing forth the divine plan for the world.

Quote 4:25

"To affect the quality of the day, that is the highest of arts. Every man is tasked to make his life, even in its details, worthy of the contemplation of his most elevated and critical hour"

- Henry David Thoreau

You can't start the next season of your life if you keep rehashing the last one. Use your past experiences as fertilizer for your future flowers. Live each day fully and give the greatest gifts to those who walk along this journey you with: choose to embrace joy, peace, freedom and love and share that with everyone.

Emerging

A slight breeze ruffles through the thought provoking scenes
As cool, quiet waves pulsate from the serene
What needs to be said, to complete the dread
What panic needs to go, to let my Spirit soar

Creeping in from the well of memories
Masked by the silent films of past stories
The breath brings longing from places unknown
Torn by the rippling of things rarely shown

Looking deep into the crater of my heart's longing
Littered with leaves inscribed with wise knowing
There I find your hand in mine
Giving me a long awaited sign

Lifting me to new journeys of ecstatic teaching
Dissolving the repetitive visions of reaching, searching, creeping
Shifting the focus to cellular rebirth
Emerging with energized streams of long lost worth

Grateful for the fine-tuned inner ear
The swirling of possibilities wrought with no fear
Songs of joy oscillate in the still beyond
Allowing the inner dancer to respond

- Denise Loy Buchanan
November 12, 2004

Author Quotes

www.ingramcontent.com/pod-product-compliance
Lightning Source LLC
Chambersburg PA
CBHW020537290526
45786CB00002B/918